THE SUPINE COBBLER

A PLAY BY JILL CONNELL

Coach House Books | Toronto

first edition

For production rights inquiries, contact Jill Connell, It Could Still Happen, jill@itcouldstillhappen.com.

Canadä

Published with the generous assistance of the Canada Council for the Arts and the Ontario Arts Council. Coach House Books also acknowledges the support of the Government of Canada through the Canada Book Fund and the Government of Ontario through the Ontario Book Publishing Tax Credit.

LIBRARY AND ARCHIVES CANADA CATALOGUING IN PUBLICATION

Connell, Jill, 1976-, author
The supine cobbler / Jill Connell.

A play.
Issued in print and electronic formats.
ISBN 978-1-55245-344-5 ·

I. Title.

PS8605.O5636S96 2017 C812'.6 C2017-900096-9

The Supine Cobbler is available as an ebook: ISBN 978 1 77056 492 3 (EPUB), 978 1 77056 493 0 (PDF).

Purchase of the print version of this book entitles you to a free digital copy. To claim your ebook of this title, please email sales@chbooks.com with proof of purchase. (Coach House Books reserves the right to terminate the free digital download offer at any time.)

for ishan davé

and my parents
linda & barry

y para las niñas

Playwright's Note

I had an abortion at the Ottawa Morgentaler Clinic in June 2011. I had just graduated from the National Theatre School of Canada's playwriting program. I flew to Iceland the next day and lived in a fishing village, working with children and writing. Two months later, I flew to Fredericton, New Brunswick, where the first reading of some early writing took place – what I then called *The Abortion*.

I grew up watching Westerns, especially the revisionist Westerns. I studied antiheroes and outsiders. For a long time I wanted to be a man when I grew up. I wanted to be a person with a story. Westerns are gritty and unapologetic when it comes to life and death. They have swagger and emotional range. They deal in landscape – interior, social, and natural. I wanted to use this classic male storytelling genre to tell a hero myth for girls.

Abortion is a prevalent procedure but goes largely unseen. I was struck by how it is a decisive action – a reckoning with the self, yet very much in relationship to others, and to society. The opposite of an erasure, it takes you forward in time. I am interested in the information that comes to us through the body. The procedure is the height of acknowledgment that the abortion is real. I set out to put this action onstage.

This play took four years to create. It was, I think, the hardest thing I've tried to make. Many of my collaborators joined me very early on and are central to this play's existence. Still, it was, at times, solitary, harsh work. The more I worked on this play, the more I felt like an outsider. Making this play also broke my heart. I stand by it the same way I stand by my abortion: with deep association and affection for my choices, but, also, a kind of astonishment and sadness.

I wrote this play for five women because I was interested in what would happen if there were only female voices speaking onstage. I had rarely experienced this in the theatre and I wondered how it would feel. *The Supine Cobbler* mentions only notorious men – a reflection of the stories that continue to dominate our culture. Yet it is profoundly not about them. My political motivation was to put an abortion procedure onstage without commentary; to give voice to women without commentary. To let these things simply be.

Directing this play was not the original plan and I'm not sure that's how I would describe what I did. I could not hold all the edges of this piece. Luckily, I did not have to. I created this play for and with the women who originally performed it. It is a piece about chaos and disappointment and loneliness and desire, and it works best when it goes faster than us. I get a lot of joy out of things I do not fully understand. This way I can keep thinking about them for a long time.

In order to stage this play I worked closely with Montréal choreographer Tedi Tafel. We prioritized a physical practice based on listening and impulse that we then attempted to offer live. Working in this way was deeply pleasurable; it surprised me constantly. Often we didn't know how to proceed. How to deal with guns, the weather, obscuring the Cobbler's name? How to know where to stand? We created structures and containers so we could work in the unknown. It felt dangerous and vulnerable. I asked the performers to bring that feeling into their performances. The job was not to explain anything to the audience, but to follow the story and their impulses within it. We could not assume to understand the moment before it arrived. Things change in an instant.

To support this practice, our technical elements were operated live. Lights were moved and focused by the performers and stage manager. Music was a live band. Our venue was a warehouse by the lakeshore in Toronto. The sound of trains permeated the building every five to ten minutes. This was all part of the deal. We did not attempt to repeat the same thing twice. Some things would succeed and some would fail. We accepted this so that the piece might succeed as a whole, as an offering that was alive.

The Supine Cobbler is an ensemble piece. It is a contemporary clinical abortion in the spirit of a Western. The Cobbler has the abortion. She is our centre. This is her experience. The performers do not leave. They stay to witness, and to hold the space for this event. This is the audience's role, too.

This is a play about love. It is about trying to have integrity in a world you don't understand. We live in lawless times. Things are exquisite and devastating and totally normal. But you cannot abandon the world, so you write this experience down. You gather people around it, you try things, you invite an audience, you keep trying. It is true and flawed and we attend to this.

The task of embodying these characters is beyond what can be written in words. Different information is accessed in the body, in an ensemble, and in the act of public witness. This text is a map for finding that.

Jill Connell
January 2017

Production History

The Supine Cobbler premiered in the Clay & Paper Theatre warehouse space at 35 Strachan Avenue in Toronto, Ontario, September 2015. It was produced by It Could Still Happen with the following cast and crew:

The Cobbler: Katie Swift
The Kid: Jackie Rowland
The Dancer: Chala Hunter
The Lover: Susanna Fournier
The Doctor: Leni Parker

Directed by Jill Connell
Movement and Assistance by Tedi Tafel
Dramaturgy by Brian Drader
Set and Lighting by Elizabeth Kantor
Video and Projection by Ishan Davé
Music Composition and Sound by Holger Schoorl
Stage Management by Angeline St. Amour
Technical Direction by Justis Danto-Clancy
Costumes by Jenna McCutchen
Produced by Sascha Cole and Jill Connell

The Band: Holger Schoorl, Cory Latkovich, Ishan Davé.

Also: Philip Nozuka (trailers), Tala Kamea (graphic design), Samantha Madely (photographs), Lena Suksi (drawings), Jeremy Kantor (graffiti), Amy Keating (Lindsay Hashknife), and Claudia Dey and Heidi Sopinka (select costume pieces exclusively designed by Horses Atelier).

A second production by The Maggie Tree took place in Edmonton, Alberta, April 2016, directed by Vanessa Sabourin and featuring Lora Brovold, Kristi Hansen, Jayce Mckenzie, Michelle Milenkovic, and Melissa Thingelstad.

Personajes

The Cobbler. ~~Grace Volonté Cordovan.~~ *A shoemaker and an outlaw.*

The Kid. Everett 'the Kid' McMurtrett-Howley-Réjean-Cournoyer. *The Cobbler's apprentice.*

The Dancer / Nurse 1. Frankie (Francisca) Cordovan. *The Cobbler's older sister.*

The Lover / Nurse 2. Leigh Meloné. *The Cobbler's best friend.*

The Doctor. Name unknown. *The Cobbler's abortion provider.*

Setting

Present day, present city.

Locations that distill and morph:

1. The Theatre
2. The Wilderness
3. The Abortion Clinic
4. The City

Mood and landscape are supreme in the Western.

Physical Things

That which is elemental (fire, water, earth, plant, animal) or enfranchises action (digging, hanging, sitting, chopping, dressing).

Objects can be replaced by reading a stage direction, stating that you have an object, or feeling like you have an object.

Text

A slash indicates overlap. A strikethrough indicates something we are not allowed to hear. The text both is exacting and invites improvisation.

What to Wear

This is a contemporary Western. Hats and boots are important. Animal: leather, feather, fur. Accessories: kerchiefs, suspenders, charms. The women dress for the wilderness (changeable), more than the heat. They are fashionable, as outlaws tend to be.

Otras Cosas

The ensemble is always onstage, as players or as witness.

Sound is a live band. They play throughout, or they witness.

The technical elements are transparent. A performer-operated light can choose what it illuminates. We trade theatre magic for aliveness.

The film genre can be evoked throughout; however, the final film is the only film in the play.

The show is changeable. That which is repeatable and essential anchors that which is untamable and unknown.

The Cobbler is our centre; the play moves around her.

The Doctor is our wild card and our host. She can be used to solve most artistic challenges.

While the Dancer and Lover might be dead or missing, they must first be present and returned, with real demands and real bodies.

The Kid sees everything. She is heroic and sane, along with the rest of them.

It is both. Both contemporary and a Western. Both a clinic and the wild. Both objective and subjective. Both true story and legend. Stories, myths, histories are always thus. We can only see from our own eye(s).

The Supine Cobbler

The audience enters. There is a bar where they can buy tall cans of beer and whisky in real glasses. A Fistful of Dollars *plays on the* TV *screen, sound muted. Music plays: contemporary, female, popular.*

The DANCER, LOVER, *and* KID *sit at the bar. The* DOCTOR *observes from a distance. They wear dusters.*

The Doctor nods. It's time. Music quiets. House lights dim. The bartender settles up with any customers. Musicians take their places.

TV *sound from* A Fistful of Dollars *comes in. It is the final duel of the film. The Dancer, Lover, and Kid watch. At the height of the duel: the* TV *cuts out. House lights out.*

The palpable expectation of silence. The band strikes a resonant chord.

The COBBLER *enters. She stands at the threshold wearing a duster.*

The three at the bar turn. Eyes meet with the Cobbler's. A small lifetime in this gaze.

The Cobbler approaches the bar.

The bartender pours four shots of whisky. They drink: a sober yet casual complicity.

Prologue

The Doctor addresses the audience.

DOCTOR: You all remember the year we had no rain. The year Hassan Jarrar beat a hooker into a coma, same year as the HIV hate-mongering, fifty-three homicides, 243 suicides, that we know of in this city. Almost twenty years ago now. Same year the Cordovan house burnt clean to the ground in the middle of the night, mother and father inside. Two daughters camped in a tent nearby, twelve and fourteen – these the remains of the tragedy. The elder daughter got sent to the Winnipeg Ballet, while the younger took over the family business. Became a shoemaker. She grew into a nice, middle-of-the-road, nice, respectable, nice young woman. Well, not nice, but decent. Then one day she just fell off the map of decency. In the public eye. In the opinion of civilized society. You've heard the rumours. The Supine Cobbler, this and that. People talk. The Hashknives, the Nacogdoches, they talk. Now you and I keep quiet. Even though we know a lot of things. We keep quiet. Still. Nobody knows this here story I'm about to unfold. Nobody talks about this. Even though it happened this year. Ultimately this story is brutal and unforgiving. Pretty violent and heartbreaking overall. That's because most of what follows is true.

Powder flash. Dusters drop to the ground. Lights expose the gang in a criminal line-up. They step forward one by one as their photographs are taken.

Francisca Cordovan, AKA Frankie. Thirty-three. The Cobbler's older sister. Achieved some small fame as a dancer in the Winnipeg Ballet. Met her death by hanging. One tough son of a bitch, such is the way with dancers of the ballet.

Leigh Meloné. Twenty-nine. The Cobbler's best friend. Just friends. Married to the Kestrel. He's not the topic. Leigh went missing three or four years ago, leaving not so much as footprints in the snow, presumed dead.

Everett 'the Kid' McMurtrett-Howley-Réjean-Cournoyer. Twenty-two. The Cobbler's apprentice. Man-woman-child, a charmer, turncoat, as it turns out. Lived down the street from the Cordovans. Still does.

~~Grace Volonté Cordovan.~~ Thirty-something with no name. Well, she was thirty-one and she had a name but you wouldn't recognize it. I'm not going to try to explain her, as that would be a disservice, and tonight's soirée would not be needed if I could. But she was a plain genius, with a concern for doing the right thing. And that's where the trouble begins.

This is the story of one particular event, one particular sally into the wilderness. I was there for some of it. Some good times we felt immortal but also some mix-ups. Half of them end up dead. At least half.

Gotta know what kind of funeral you want.

Silence.

A morning bird.

LOVER: What are you thinking about?

COBBLER: Lovin'.

Gunshot. Blackout.

Horses' hooves morph into a train at full steam: loud. Or: an adventure song.

One: Waiting Room

Clinic door shuts. Clinic lights up on clinic chairs. Clinic eighties music: filtered, one world in remove. The Cobbler and Kid stand arrived. The Kid has the Cobbler's bag slung over her shoulder.

Punctuated by silences:

KID: Is this the place?

COBBLER: Yeah. What time is it?

The Kid carries the Cobbler's smashed iPhone. She checks it.

KID: 7:15. What time's our appointment?

COBBLER: Noon.

KID: Maybe we're early.

COBBLER: We're supposed to come early.

KID: Who's that person?

COBBLER: Doctor.

KID: You know her?

COBBLER: No.

DOCTOR: You can have a seat.

They go to sit.

Hang your coat and hats.

They do.

Sit. It's a waiting room.

They sit. They wait.

The Doctor removes her duster. Underneath she wears underwear and a soccer jersey that says GIRLS *or* MARADONA *on the back. She transforms over the course of the play toward her role in the procedure.*

Crickets. Waiting.

The Doctor puts a wolf pelt on the clothesline and travels it over to the waiting room. The Cobbler and Kid watch the wolf. The Doctor sits at her vanity smoking a water-vapour cigarette.

Punctuated by silences:

KID: This is a lot of waiting.

COBBLER: It's been about two minutes.

KID: You think we'll have to live here forever?

COBBLER: No, it's just a checkup.

KID: You think she'll know what you have?

COBBLER: Yeah.

KID: I don't want to live here forever.

COBBLER: We'll leave today.

KID: At least it's not raining. At least we're not starving. At least we don't live in a palace. Did I say palace? I meant a townhouse. At least we don't live in a townhouse beside a Walmart. Prison's going to be bad. It's going to be like prison. But at least we'll have a place to live. What do you think you have?

COBBLER: Nothing, really. I bet it's really common.

KID: Do you think I have it too?

COBBLER: No.

KID: It feels like I have it.

COBBLER: You don't have it.

KID: I hope you don't have something that costs a lot of money to fix. I hope you don't have something that once you have it everyone hates you. I hope you have something so common there's no name for it, something so common we don't have to fix it because everyone has it.

COBBLER: Yes.

KID: Things could be worse. Still, things feel pretty bad. Which means they can only get better. Until we have to go to prison.

COBBLER: We're not going to go to prison.

KID: I'm going to prison. I'm going to prison like five times.

COBBLER: I'll tell your parents.

KID: I'll tell my parents. Things are going to get so bad for me.

The Cobbler looks at the Kid.

I think this is a wolf. / Skin. Pelt.

COBBLER: / I think so.

KID: I want to put it on.

COBBLER: I think it's art.

KID: Shit, she's coming over.

The Doctor enters.

DOCTOR: Let's see your ID.

The Cobbler gets her wallet from the Kid.

Two pieces.

The Cobbler gives the Doctor two cards. The Doctor returns a card.

This is expired. Health card.

The Cobbler gives the Doctor her health card.

You must be the shoemaker.

COBBLER: I'm his daughter.

DOCTOR: You're not the shoemaker?

COBBLER: Yes. My dad was the original shoemaker, like a true maker of shoes. That's what he did. There's some confusion. I am also a shoemaker.

DOCTOR: Yeah, well, you are what you do.

COBBLER: Or don't do.

DOCTOR: No. You are not what you don't do.

COBBLER: Well, I mostly make boots.

DOCTOR: Cordovan, what's that / Spanish?

COBBLER: / Spanish. Extraction. It is. However, my first given name is after a quality my parents hoped I would embody and my middle given name is after my father, who was named after my grandmother's lover, who was a film actor in the Westerns. The Italian Westerns.

DOCTOR: I prefer the originals.

COBBLER: Some people do.

DOCTOR: Kurosawa.

COBBLER: Some people don't consider those the originals.

DOCTOR: You speak Spanish?

COBBLER: It comes to me when I need it.

DOCTOR: *Yo chingué a tu madre.* I fucked your mother. That's all I know how to say.

COBBLER: My mother was from New Brunswick.

DOCTOR: I grew up in New Brunswick.

An improvisation where the Cobbler and Doctor continue about New Brunswick until a commonality is found. Perhaps a common thing they don't know – the Cobbler has never been.

I'd like to go back but I'm afraid of getting shot. I wear a bullet-proof vest – rabbit and Kevlar. I'll show you later. I'm going to need you to fill out these forms. I'm going to call in your health card and eat a power bar.

Who's this?

COBBLER: This is Everett the Kid.

KID: How do you do.

DOCTOR: I don't want any trouble around here.

COBBLER: She's very reliable.

DOCTOR: Good for you.

The Doctor goes.

COBBLER: (*to Kid*) It's okay.

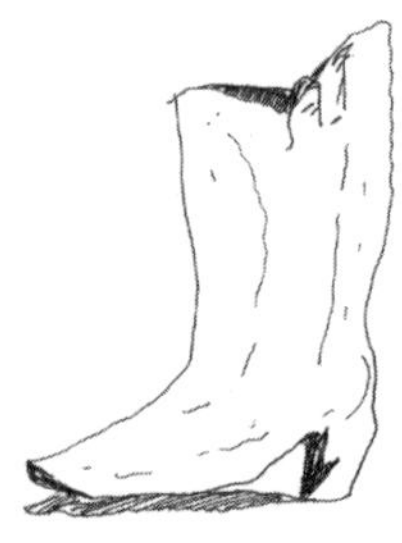

Two: Return of my Sister

The Cobbler and Kid sit in clinic chairs. The Cobbler fills out forms. The Kid flips through a fashion magazine.

The crickets quiet abruptly. The Cobbler and the Kid pause. The Dancer's refrain enters briefly. The Kid turns her head to the side. It's gone.

The crickets resume. The Cobbler and Kid resume: forms, magazine.

The Dancer approaches at a steady pace. The Cobbler and the Kid listen, on alert as if being hunted.

Creak of door hinges. The Cobbler and Kid rise to standing, backs toward the door.

The Dancer stands arrived.

All three stand at ready, face front.

DANCER: I'm looking for the shoemaker.

COBBLER: He's not here.

DANCER: I'm not looking for a man. I'm looking for his disciple. ~~Grace Volunté Cordovan~~. You heard of her?

COBBLER: No, what's she like?

DANCER: Well let me tell you. She makes the most beautiful shoes, been making shoes since she was a kid, real perfectionist as a girl, real detail-oriented, real temper, get so worked up people had to sit on her 'til she calm down. One eye.

COBBLER: She sounds nice, now if you don't mind ...

DANCER: Sure. Sure. I don't mind. No problem, sure.

The Dancer walks forward. She removes her boots.

DANCER: *¿Ves éstas botas?* (See these boots?)

COBBLER: *Veo esas botas.* (I see those boots.)

No one looks at the boots.

DANCER: *¿Quién las hizo?* (Who made them?)

COBBLER: *Yo las hice.* (I did.)

The Kid looks at the boots.

Sonny.

The Kid looks away from the boots.

DANCER: *Te reconocería en mis sueños aunque no te haya visto en diecinueve años.* (I'd recognize you in my sleep even though I haven't seen you in nineteen years.) Here's a letter for you.

The Cobbler already has the letter.

COBBLER: Thank you.

DANCER: It's from me.

COBBLER: I know.

The Kid goes to move.

COBBLER: Sonny, I'm having a conversation!

Silence.

Something about this letter makes me feel like even if I read it it'll already be too late.

BOTH: C'mere.

A negotiation:

–You c'mere.
–No you c'mere.

Until:

DANCER: / Meet you halfway.

COBBLER: / Okay.

They approach.

COBBLER: Let me see your feet.
This permanent?

DANCER: Ingrown toenail.

COBBLER: Corns.

DANCER: Yeah, I cut them off once in a while.
Surgery.

COBBLER: Yep, that's surgery.

DANCER: Yeah. This is a ganglion.

COBBLER: See this – this knuckle out of line, can't barely bend it. That's nothin', just dry. Can't feel this whole palm. Slap it.

The Dancer does.

Harder.

The Dancer does.

Harder.

The Dancer slaps her very hard.

See, can't feel that.

DANCER: From making shoes?

The Cobbler cracks her knuckles.

COBBLER: Naw, I punched a whatchacallit, hydro pole.

DANCER: Hear that?

COBBLER: Don't touch the back of my head.

The Dancer is not.

DANCER: Hear that?

The Dancer's hip can be heard without her even moving.

Fucked-up hip. Every time. I do anything. See this? Dead tooth, need a root canal on this whole side of my face. Full canal.

An improvisation where the Cobbler and Dancer compare injuries: the real and the invented. A growing sibling rivalry, until:

COBBLER: See this? This eye?

The sisters lock eyes.

Don't work right. My sister run me through.

DANCER: Huh.

COBBLER: She was in the ballet.

DANCER: Was she now?

Sí. They nod together.

She do that on purpose?

COBBLER: I don't know. Used to call me *tuerto*. Means blind in one eye. She was a fucking dance genius.

DANCER: / Listen.

COBBLER: / I'm listening.

DANCER: I had a dream / about you last night.

COBBLER: / Don't tell me your dream.

DANCER: We were camped out in the backyard in a tent and you bolted up in your sleeping bag and were like:

House on fire. A moment of true panic:

COBBLER: Where are we?

DANCER: Hello!

Cut fire.

We are here.

COBBLER: I have the same dream.

The Doctor is there.

DOCTOR: Here's your health card.

COBBLER: Thank you. I need a few more minutes with the forms.

The Doctor nods. She looks at the Dancer. Back at the Cobbler.

DOCTOR: Weather's going to change.

Nodding. The Doctor goes.

DANCER: Read the letter.

COBBLER: No.

DANCER: Okay.

The Dancer begins digging her grave.

Thunderheads in the distance.

COBBLER: Let's set up camp.

KID: Okay. I'm going to go do my thing.

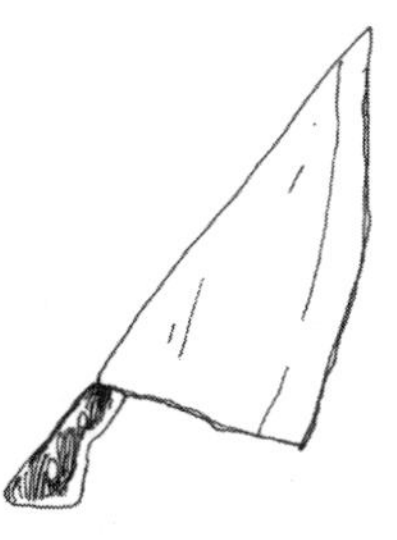

Three: Leigh Meloné

The Kid sets up a tent. Pale parachute silk, guy lines high, not necessarily tent-like. Throughout this scene the Kid sources water, sweeps, mops, folds clothes, and builds a fire.

The Cobbler sits alone in the clinic.

The Lover appears in the clinic chair beside her.

Silence. They do not meet eyes.

COBBLER: Fancy meeting you here.

LOVER: Fancy meeting you here.

COBBLER: Back in town?

LOVER: No.

COBBLER: Long time no see.

LOVER: Yep.

COBBLER: Yep.

LOVER: You dressin' like a girl now?

COBBLER: No.

LOVER: You makin' friends?

COBBLER: No.

LOVER: Who's that?

COBBLER: She's a dancer.

LOVER: Cool. What's this place?

COBBLER: Doctor's.

LOVER: You sick?

COBBLER: Nope.

The Lover nods.

LOVER: You get my letters?

COBBLER: What letters?

LOVER: Yeah, I guess I didn't send any letters.

COBBLER: No, I guess not.

DANCER: She's got a letter from me.

LOVER: You got a letter from her?

DANCER: She won't read it.

LOVER: No?

COBBLER: No.

DANCER: It's a suicide letter.

LOVER: Ah.

The Kid enters. The Lover draws on the Kid. The Dancer and Cobbler draw guns. The Kid does not have a gun. Tense moment.

COBBLER: Kid. Kid.

KID: Yeah.

The Kid snaps out of it.

COBBLER: Go do your thing.

KID: I'm going to go do my thing.

The Kid goes.

The Dancer continues with her grave.

LOVER: (*the Kid*) Who's that?

COBBLER: She's my new best friend.

LOVER: I wanted to call but I didn't pay my phone.

COBBLER: Right.

LOVER: It's not like you didn't know where I was.

COBBLER: I had no idea where you were!

LOVER: I was in fucking hiding.

COBBLER: Yeah, where's that?

LOVER: Out by the tracks.

COBBLER: What tracks?

LOVER: Tracks by the place. Train tracks.

COBBLER: Yeah, I don't know where that is.

LOVER: It's hidden. So?

COBBLER: What?

LOVER: What.

COBBLER: What.

LOVER: What are you asking there?

COBBLER: What are you hiding from?

LOVER: Well, I would ask you the same question.

The Lover unfurls the Cobbler's Wanted poster.

COBBLER: Rightly so.

LOVER: Crossed the creek in two different places on my way here. Cover my tracks.

COBBLER: That's a nice picture. Nice picture of me in my hat.

LOVER: Yeah, you haven't seen that? It's everywhere.

COBBLER: I'm not really on the internet right now.

DANCER: (*to Cobbler, re: poster*) Is that my hat?

COBBLER: I'd rather be wanted by something real, like a person, as opposed to like ...

LOVER: The Law.

COBBLER: Yeah, like a concept.

LOVER: Yeah.

COBBLER: This should say 'Unwanted.' Like, wanted for what?

LOVER: Wanted for dead.

COBBLER: Wanted for five hundred bucks. They don't even know my name.

LOVER: Yeah, it's not that great to be wanted.

COBBLER: Yeah, I don't find it that compelling.

LOVER: What's the charge?

COBBLER: Fuckin' ... who knows. I haven't really talked to them.

LOVER: This says 'dangerous.'

DANCER: (*to anyone who will listen*) That's my hat.

COBBLER: Yeah ... I don't know why they'd think that. I think most of the charges are just ideas ... idea-based ... and general petty criminality ... small time, below standard ... just, general things you shouldn't do.

LOVER: I see.

COBBLER: Getting on the wrong side of ...

LOVER: The Law.

COBBLER: Yeah, not just that. I think also, like ... The People.

LOVER: The People.

COBBLER: Yeah that's it.

LOVER: That's it?

COBBLER: Yeah.

The Kid passes by. Wait a minute. She backs up.

KID: Is this a Wanted poster?

COBBLER: Yes.

KID: This is you.

COBBLER: Yes.

KID: This says five hundred bucks.

COBBLER: I know.

KID: That's a lot of money.

COBBLER: Not really once you're older.

KID: Your face is on a poster.

COBBLER: Kid.

KID: I'm going to go do my thing.

The Kid goes.

COBBLER: Where's Maxine?

LOVER: She was in a car accident. Lost a leg.

COBBLER: What?

LOVER: I didn't see her.

COBBLER: Jesus.

LOVER: Yeah. My luck ran out.

COBBLER: You're a terrible driver.

LOVER: Naw. You can't even drive.

COBBLER: Anyone can tell.

LOVER: I'd been drinking, too, so.

COBBLER: Shit. Which leg?

LOVER: (*a back leg*) This one.

COBBLER: Is that a good one?

LOVER: Not really.

COBBLER: Shit.

LOVER: Yeah, it's not pretty. I knew you'd be sad if I didn't bring her. She couldn't come all this way, had to cross the creek twice in two different places.

COBBLER: Why are you crossing the creek like that?

LOVER: Cover my tracks. I lead to you and vice versa. We'd be two sardines in a grave. Anyway. Maxine's back at camp with my kid.

COBBLER: You have a kid?

LOVER: Yep.

COBBLER: What kind?

LOVER: Three-year-old person. A girl.

COBBLER: What's her name?

LOVER: ~~Grace Volonté Cordovan.~~ Same as yours.

The Doctor is there.

DOCTOR: Hey.

LOVER: Hey.

DOCTOR: Can I have those forms?

COBBLER: Yes.

The Doctor scans the forms in silence.

LOVER: Well. We're gonna figure this out.

COBBLER: What?

LOVER: All of this.

COBBLER: Oh yeah?

LOVER: Everything. You and me.

COBBLER: Yeah, when's that?

LOVER: Right now.

COBBLER: I can't right now.

LOVER: Why not?

COBBLER: I got a thing to do.

LOVER: Oh yeah? What thing?

DOCTOR: I'll be back.

The Doctor goes.

COBBLER: Nothing I care to talk about right now.

LOVER: When's all this nothing happening?

COBBLER: Right now.

LOVER: All right then.

COBBLER: You're not going to stick around?

LOVER: I'll stick around. (*the Dancer*) She sticking around?

COBBLER: Likely so.

LOVER: What kind of boots are you wearing?

COBBLER: I don't know.

KID: (*lighting the campfire*) Fire! Everybody watch out! Fire in the hole!

LOVER: Who is that?

COBBLER: She's my helper.
(*to Dancer*) You remember Everett?

DANCER: No.

COBBLER: Yeah, you remember the kid from down the street, that big house with the pool with that deck on top of the carport? Big sculpture.

DANCER: Yeah?

COBBLER: It's like six doors down. She had a brother.

DANCER: Oh yeah. He had that friend from Burlington who shaved his whole body.

COBBLER: I don't know.

DANCER: Yeah everything. He was a swimmer. Lane swimmer.

COBBLER: Well, she's his sister. The sister of the brother.

DANCER: I don't remember her.

COBBLER: Yeah, she wasn't of consequence to us then.

DANCER: And now?

COBBLER: Now she's older. She's got amazing reflexes.

The Kid proves this.

LOVER: How'd you two hook up?

COBBLER: By random. Same place same time.

DANCER: She lives down the street.

COBBLER: I took her on as my apprentice. She's good. And I use their bathroom. It's just nicer than the outhouse. Our real house burnt down so I live in the shoemaking studio if you'll recall.

The Lover and Dancer know.

I'm pregnant.

LOVER: Congratulations.

COBBLER: Thank you.

DANCER: I heard that.

LOVER: Yeah, me too.

Nodding. We all heard that.

DANCER: Lindsay Hashknife.

COBBLER: I know.

DANCER: She's calling you the Supine Cobbler.

COBBLER: Yes, I heard that. It is a ridiculous moniker.

DANCER: The video is likewise ridiculous.

LOVER: They banned me for my comments.

COBBLER: What video?

Pause.

I really haven't been on the internet.

LOVER: Kid, you got the internet?

The Kid does. The Lover, Dancer, and Cobbler gather around the phone and screen a YouTube video. Over the video, an improvisation where the Lover and Dancer explain to the Cobbler how this type of gossip works. They can stop the video at any time.

LINDSAY HASHKNIFE VOICE-OVER: Namaste, beautiful yogis, my name is Lindsay Hashknife and today I'll be teaching you Supta Baddha Konasana or the Supine Cobbler. 'Supine' means a person lying recumbent on their back. And here we go. Thighs open to the skies. You'll notice this is a position where you want to offer very little resistance. Your body feels torpid and lifeless. Clear the mind. 'Supine' also means failing to act as a result of moral weakness or indolence, a kind of spineless, submissive person. Breathe from your belly. Did you know, speaking of cobblers, that I used to be friends with the Cordovans? I was best friends with their youngest daughter, ~~Grace Volonté Cordovan.~~ I basically grew up in their house, the one that burnt down. Soften your inner ears. I knew her parents. And her sister. Now deceased. Breathe in and out. Little smile on your face. Let this pose move through your body. The Supine Cobbler. Open your heart chakra: send her love, passion, acceptance.

COBBLER: Okay.

DANCER: We should have killed her when we had the chance.

Nodding.

LOVER: So you're having a kid?

COBBLER: No sir. I don't think so, no.

Nodding.

DANCER: I've not had a kid before. In Paris.

LOVER: Once I didn't have a kid twice in one year.

The Cordovan sisters raise one eyebrow each.

Yeah.

COBBLER: You have a great capacity.

LOVER: Yeah. Also I was pretty disorganized at the time.

The Kid coming.

COBBLER: I haven't told her yet.

The Kid joins them.

COBBLER: Kid, I want to introduce you.

KID: Okay.

COBBLER: This is my old friend, Leigh Meloné. I present you Everett the Kid.

KID: How do you do.

LOVER: How do you do.

COBBLER: This is my sister, Frankie Cordovan. Everett the Kid.

KID: How do you do.

DANCER: How do you do.

LOVER: This is your sister?

COBBLER: Yeah, this is Frankie.

LOVER: She's your sister?

COBBLER: Yes. This is my sister.

LOVER: This is your sister?

COBBLER: Yes. This is my sister. This is Frankie.

DANCER: Is something funny?

COBBLER: No.

LOVER: Kid, I'll take a coffee.

KID: Okay.

LOVER: (*to Dancer*) I like your clothes.

DANCER: Thank you.

LOVER: (*Cobbler's boots*) Are those synthetic?

COBBLER: Yeah, they're from Payless.

LOVER: You're a shoemaker.

COBBLER: Yes and I have to make shoes for other people. I have to make a living.

LOVER: At the expense of your values?

COBBLER: I think so, yes.

DANCER: I've got Cordovan originals.

KID: Me too.

LOVER: Yeah, me too.

They compare Cordovan originals.

DOCTOR: ~~Grace Volonté Cordovan.~~

COBBLER: Excuse me.

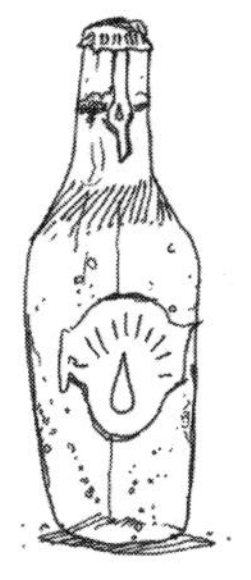

Four: Counselling

DOCTOR: This is counselling: make sure you're behind your decision, discuss birth control, offer you optional pre-op drugs.

COBBLER: Okay.

DOCTOR: Are you confident about your decision?

COBBLER: Yes. It's a good decision for me. You need to hear my reasons?

DOCTOR: No. So long as they're yours.

COBBLER: They are.

DOCTOR: Good. Let's discuss protection.

COBBLER: I know about protection.

DOCTOR: It's good to use protection.

COBBLER: Yes, thank you. Some days that just seems more impossible than others.

DOCTOR: I have to check in on whether you have a plan for the future –

COBBLER: I do not have a plan for the future.

DOCTOR: In terms of birth control.

COBBLER: I do not.

A lesson on taking positive action:

DOCTOR: One time I found a lump in my breast and took it out. Breast surgery. Wasn't cancer. Positive action.

COBBLER: Yeah, but you're a doctor.

DOCTOR: Yeah? You know what I'm not? A tattoo artist. Check

this out: (*her full back*) I'm showing you my tattoo. I gave this to myself. See that? I'm pointing to something I drew myself.

COBBLER: That's good. Sorry. I can't tell if it was or wasn't cancer.

DOCTOR: Wasn't cancer.

COBBLER: So you never had cancer.

DOCTOR: Whether it's cancer or not cancer, you have to do something with your life. Not something impressive, just literally something. The time has to pass somehow.

COBBLER: I'm doing something right now.

DOCTOR: That's good.

COBBLER: Listen, Doc. Can I call you Doc?

DOCTOR: Doc's fine.

COBBLER: Listen, Doc. We've just met. Don't tell me I'm doing good.

Beat.

DOCTOR: I've got some optional pre-op drugs. One milligram of Ativan and 600 milligrams of ibuprofen.

COBBLER: That's a lot of ibuprofen.

DOCTOR: It's not.

COBBLER: What do people normally take?

DOCTOR: Normally people take them both.

COBBLER: I'll take them for later.

DOCTOR: That's not possible.

COBBLER: Fine, I'll pass.

DOCTOR: Fine. Go get changed.

COBBLER: Okay.

The Doctor goes.

The Cobbler travels the space, getting up and down from supine, often on the edge of stillness. She is in silent conversation with the scene below.

Meanwhile, the Kid, Dancer, and Lover shuck corn onto newspaper.

KID: I'll do all these corns for twenty bucks.

LOVER: No way.

KID: But I need money.

LOVER: How much money you got?

KID: We share.

LOVER: You don't have your own money?

The Kid doesn't.

How much has she got?

KID: I think we have six dollars for the bus.

LOVER: Okay. Yeah, you need money.

DANCER: You need a job.

KID: I have jobs, just no one pays me.

LOVER: Yeah, she needs money. Not jobs, money.

DANCER: Or a career.

LOVER: A career is good if you can get one.

KID: Like shoemaking.

LOVER: Sure, and if you can't get a career there are things you just have. Once I almost sold my kidneys, one kidney.

KID: Why didn't you?

LOVER: I didn't know you had to be knocked out. I was knocked out once at a party in high school. It's no good. Kidneys aren't a job, they're something you've got. You can sell your eggs.

DANCER: What if she wants to have kids?

LOVER: She can still have kids. You want to have kids?

KID: Yeah, I'll have kids but I'd rather have, like, leprosy. Or I'd rather have, like, a garden, a really elaborate garden.

LOVER: Same problem, though, with the eggs – you have to be knocked out. It's no good.

KID: I'll have a garden or leprosy or kids when I'm older. But not kids.

DANCER: You think that'd be more trendy.

The Lover and the Dancer riff on current/global instances of sexual violence and environmental change, respectively.

LOVER: It's very trendy. Bus gang rape, football-high-school-college-party gang rape, cyberbulling gang rape suicide, / rape and silence, rape and school the next day, rape and work the next day, rape and public humiliation, rape and social sanction, casual rape comments at parties that result in actual rape. Once you stop drinking you notice this a lot.

DANCER: / I mean not having kids. What with the impending world water crisis, ice caps melting, drought and food shortages, drought and displacement, people drowning trying to escape their country, people dead in shipping containers, humanitarian crisis, Syria.

KID: Yeah, I haven't heard of that. I just need some money.

DANCER: You haven't heard of Syria?

LOVER: Over there they get guns when they're, like, five. That's fucked up but you know what I got when I was five? (*equally fucked*) A Popple.

(*Dancer's corn*) You about done with that?

KID: What's a Popple?

The Dancer finishes her corn adeptly and drops it in the pot.

DANCER: I'm going to eat that later.

The Dancer travels the space, her body acutely alive, searching for a grave. She is in silent conversation with her sister and the scene below.

LOVER: Kid.

Hey Kid.

KID: Yes.

LOVER: What's your name again?

KID: Everett.

LOVER: Everett. Is that a boy's name?

KID: Yes. My parents didn't know that.

LOVER: What's your last name?

KID: I don't really use it.

LOVER: Yeah, but what is it?

KID: McMurtrett-Howley-Réjean-Cournoyer.

The Kid spits.

LOVER: A Popple is like a fucking bear or like this rabbit with a long tail that has a pouch on its back and it can go inside the pouch and turn into a ball of fur, a furball. It's like a mutated Care Bear. One Christmas I got a Popple from my Mom and my Dad – two Popples. Your parents together?

KID: Yes.

LOVER: That's rare.

KID: Yeah, it's rare.

The Kid spits again.

What's a Care Bear?

LOVER: How'd you learn to spit like that?

KID: My brother. He had a vasectomy. Not a vasectomy – well, he had a vasectomy but also a ... bowel resection surgery.

Beat.

LOVER: You have a gun?

KID: No.

LOVER: You share one.

KID: I'm not allowed.

LOVER: Take one of mine. I've got two.

The Lover gives the Kid a gun.

The Lover and Kid square off. They draw. The Kid's not bad.

Here's the key to making money: you're not above anything and you're qualified for everything.

KID: Okay.

LOVER: What would you do for money?

KID: Anything.

LOVER: (*Kid's gun*) Put that away.
Okay. Here's the thing. You do not do unethical things for money. You do unethical things because you want to. There's a difference.

The Lover spits.

Fuck. It's no good.

KID: You're thinking about it too much. Don't think about it too much. That's the thing about my brother is he basically puts no effort into it, or into anything.

The Kid spits.

The Lover spits. It's no good.

What are you thinking about?

LOVER: My parents.

KID: Don't think about your parents. Don't think about anything.

LOVER: (*to Dancer*) Stop doing that.

DANCER: I can't.

LOVER: Why not?

DANCER: I have this weird leg thing.

LOVER: What weird lady thing?

DANCER: Leg thing.

LOVER: What weird leg thing?

DANCER: You won't have heard of it.

LOVER: Try me.

DANCER: My iliopsoas basically disconnected from my spine.

LOVER: Okay. Did you reconnect it?

DANCER: I tried. I also have osteoarthritis in all my joints.

LOVER: Doesn't everyone have that?

KID: I think my grandma has that.

DANCER: Is your grandma a ballet dancer?

KID: No.

LOVER: I bet your grandma doesn't stand like that either.

DANCER: Doesn't matter.

LOVER: It seems to matter.

DANCER: It matters if you've made ballet your life.

LOVER: Yeah, I have no idea why you'd want to do that.

DANCER: I can tell.

The Dancer abandons her body.

LOVER: One time I drove through an unmarked construction zone by mistake, thought it was just a bumpy road. Then my car caught on fire and I was so drunk I passed out in a churchyard, woke up, like, *what the fuck is on my face,* no idea where I was.

Silence.

KID: What was on your face?

LOVER: Vomit. Dried blood. Then this Coke truck drove by with a turkey on top, like in the middle of the city, a turkey on top of a Coke truck and I thought, like, *where do you think you're going?*

KID: Where were you going?

LOVER: Nowhere. But you know what else? Fuck. I forget my point. (*Beat. Got it.*) You know what else? My car was totally on fire and now you can't even tell. Point being, things repair themselves. Like your leg no one's heard of. And. I quit drinking.

The Cobbler is returned.

I quit drinking.

COBBLER: That's good.

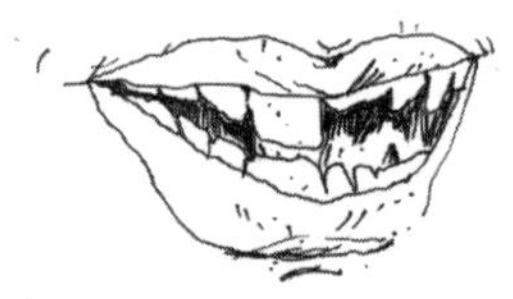

Five: #nightgown

KID: How'd it go?

COBBLER: Good. I have to get changed.

KID: Corns are ready.

COBBLER: I'm not allowed to eat.

DANCER: I'll take one.

The Kid gets supplies from the Cobbler's backpack.

KID: Nightgown.

COBBLER: I don't want to wear that.

KID: She said you have to change.

The Cobbler undresses.

You have nice veins.

COBBLER: Thank you.

KID: (*vein*) I've got this one. (*something else*) Also this thing.

COBBLER: Nice.

The Cobbler puts on the nightgown.

KID: Slippers.

COBBLER: Where'd you get those?

KID: They're my mom's.

COBBLER: I can't wear those.

KID: They're just slippers.

The Cobbler puts on the slippers.

COBBLER: Fuck I look dumb.

The Kid takes the Cobbler's picture and Instagrams it.

KID: #Ilookdumb

The Dancer is eating a cob of corn conspicuously.

LOVER: What are you doing? Why are you doing that?

COBBLER: She's got a bad tooth. Ballet dancers can withstand pain like no other.

LOVER: That's disgusting.

COBBLER: They are actually insane people.

KID: I wish I was an insane person. / Like a lawyer.

LOVER: / I can't look at her.

COBBLER: Don't look at her.

KID: Or, like, an Olympic diver. / White House person.

COBBLER: / Stop. Don't look at her.

LOVER: I can't help it.

KID: Maybe don't have corn. Just have mash.

LOVER: What's actually the problem?

KID: Mashed food.

COBBLER: Bad tooth.

LOVER: No, this is not about a bad tooth.

COBBLER: I think it's the whole area.

LOVER: You don't need to eat that. Corn actually has very little nutritional value.

KID: Maybe let the doctor see your tooth.

DANCER: No.

COBBLER: / She's not a dentist.

LOVER: / Seriously, what is actually the problem?

KID: But still.

DANCER: I said no.

KID: Why not?

LOVER: Yeah, why not?

DANCER: I don't want to look old.

COBBLER: You're not going to look old.

LOVER: You're not going to look old, you're going to look poor.

KID: I don't want to look poor.

LOVER: You're not going to look poor. (*the Dancer*) She's going to look poor.

DANCER: I don't want to fuck up my face.

KID: I want to look rich.

LOVER: Okay. I'm going to say this for your own good. Your face is already insane. Just get over it. You think I was happy when my vagina started looking bad?

COBBLER: No.

LOVER: No, I wasn't. But was it a blessing in disguise?

COBBLER: It wasn't.

LOVER: It was. One day you notice something starts going in a certain direction, then it's going in that direction for sure, then you're at the apex of that direction. That's your face right now. But after the apex, you just get used to it. You're going to become a person with no tooth and some weird type of face and you won't even remember your old face. No one will remember your old face. I close my eyes and I can't remember your old face. Close your eyes. Everybody. Close your eyes.

Everyone closes their eyes.

See? Who can remember her face? I can't remember your face. Nothing.

The Dancer opens her eyes. House on fire.

COBBLER: Where are we?

DANCER: Hello!

Cut fire. All eyes open.

Silence. The sisters look at each other.

COBBLER: You have a face like no face I've ever seen.

LOVER: Let's see your tooth. Open up.

DANCER: / Don't touch it, just see it.

LOVER: / Yep. Yeah. Let me see. Let me see it for real. Yeah. I'm no doctor-dentist but this is – what is that is fucked. This. This is, I'm not going to touch it, I just want to look, I'm not touching it – I've got it.

The Lover has pulled the Dancer's tooth.

That's a bad tooth.

KID: Let's see? Oh yeah. Bad one. The bad egg.

They all agree on the badness of the tooth.

You should get a gold tooth. Cartel.

COBBLER: Why did your vagina start looking bad?

LOVER: I don't know. Sometimes it looks good again. It's like a fucking storm watch. Things can change in an instant.

COBBLER: No, things *do* change in an instant.

LOVER: Yeah, it's the fucking Edward Snowden. It's the fucking Omar Khadr. I'm just quoting shit here.

COBBLER: It's the fucking el Niño.

LOVER: It's the fucking David Bowie.

DANCER: It's the fucking Bill C-51.

An improvisation where the gang quotes shit, the line being: 'It's the fucking (thing that changes in an instant).' The fact is: we don't control much. This builds until:

KID: It's the fucking house burns downs with your parents inside.

A redirect:

She had sex with the Kestrel. (*the Cobbler*) She. Everybody knows.

It's true.

LOVER: I know, thanks. I meant to bring that up. I don't mind. I'm just saying.

COBBLER: Okay, but you were dead, for, like, three, four years.

LOVER: Yeah. You don't do that to your best friend, especially if they're dead.

COBBLER: You always do that to your best friend, that's like the main person you do it to.

LOVER: You thought I was dead?

COBBLER: I don't know.

LOVER: You thought I would die?

COBBLER: I said I don't know. Missing women are often dead. I didn't know what to think.

Silence.

LOVER: I think you've been two-timing me.

COBBLER: You weren't even together!

LOVER: We're together! You and me! The two-timing is right here!

COBBLER: How are we together. / This is the first time we've been together in years.

LOVER: / We're together right now.

Silence.

Wasn't it good for us?

COBBLER: Never seeing each other again? No, I don't think so.

LOVER: She didn't visit. Why aren't you mad at her?

COBBLER: She was far away! You can't visit from Winnipeg.

DANCER: I was in the ballet.

Silence.

LOVER: So what did you think?

COBBLER: Of what?

LOVER: His body.

COBBLER: I didn't see it that much. We didn't get super intimate that way. We more ... I could tell he has a pretty large body.

LOVER: A large size of body.

COBBLER: I think I have a large size of body also, so.

LOVER: That's good.

COBBLER: Not large, but like, accommodating.

LOVER: Good match.

COBBLER: No no – you guys were a way better match.

LOVER: Well, we were married.

COBBLER: For immigration purposes.

LOVER: It wasn't for immigration purposes.

COBBLER: Okay.

LOVER: We're both Canadian.

COBBLER: But it was a marriage of convenience.

LOVER: What do you mean?

COBBLER: I don't know.

LOVER: What do you mean you don't know?

COBBLER: I don't know why you got married.

LOVER: Because we were in love. We had a great love story.

COBBLER: Okay.

LOVER: You don't think we had a great love story?

The Cobbler doesn't.

DANCER: I love love stories.

COBBLER: We could never get married.

LOVER: Who?

KID: She and the Kestrel.

DANCER: It's just Kestrel.

LOVER: Who are you going to marry?

KID: I'm going to have sex with the Kestrel.

LOVER: Who are you going to marry?

COBBLER: No one.

KID: Me neither.

The Doctor enters.

DOCTOR: ~~Grace Volonté Corduvan~~.

LOVER: Have fun.

COBBLER: Thank you.

LOVER: Don't have sex with anyone along the way.

Six: Physical

DOCTOR: I'm going to do a quick physical.

COBBLER: Okay.

DOCTOR: It's extra.

COBBLER: Money?

DOCTOR: Attention. I think you could use it.

COBBLER: Okay.

DOCTOR: (*slippers*) Take those off.

COBBLER: Those aren't mine.

The Doctor begins a physical exam.

DOCTOR: How's your sleep?

COBBLER: Good.

DOCTOR: How many hours do you sleep a night?

COBBLER: Three.

DOCTOR: Nightmares?

COBBLER: Yes.

DOCTOR: What of?

COBBLER: My sister and I are camped out in our backyard and I bolt up in my sleeping bag like, *Where are we*?

DOCTOR: What's your star sign?

COBBLER: Virgo.

DOCTOR: How's your period?

COBBLER: Normal.

DOCTOR: How many sexual partners?

COBBLER: One.

DOCTOR: Any allergies?

COBBLER: Soap. Harsh soaps.

DOCTOR: What shampoo do you use?

COBBLER: Head and Shoulders.

DOCTOR: Smells nice. Breathe in, and out. You smoke?

COBBLER: Yes.

DOCTOR: How many a day?

COBBLER: Two.

DOCTOR: You drink?

COBBLER: Yes.

DOCTOR: How many drinks?

COBBLER: Six a day.

DOCTOR: Let me see your tongue. You vegetarian?

COBBLER: No.

DOCTOR: Family medical history?

COBBLER: None. Early deaths.

DOCTOR: How many hours a week do you work?

COBBLER: A hundred.

DOCTOR: You relax at night?

COBBLER: Yes.

DOCTOR: What do you do to relax?

COBBLER: I look out the window.

DOCTOR: Do you exercise?

COBBLER: No.

DOCTOR: How do you get that body?

COBBLER: I'm a tradesman.

DOCTOR: How many pushups can you do?

COBBLER: I don't know. Fifty.

DOCTOR: Let's see.

COBBLER: The pushups.

DOCTOR: Yeah. Let's see them.

The Cobbler does pushups: a spectator event.

DOCTOR: That was seventy-four. What's your sense of reality?

COBBLER: Good.

DOCTOR: Yeah?

COBBLER: (*nodding*) What do you mean by reality?

DOCTOR: The world as it is.

COBBLER: Versus the world as it seems to me? Because I can't see that well. (*her eye*) See this? My sister stabbed me. With her fist.

The Dancer has a juvenile reaction.

What?

DANCER: That eye never worked.

The Cobbler has a juvenile reaction.

Oh my god. Get over it. That eye never worked and you know it. / That's right. I'm older. I remember. *Tuerto.* That eye always sucked since you were a baby.

COBBLER: / I'm over it. Okay. I'm over it. But I've only got one good eye. Don't call me that. Whisperer.

The Cobbler puts on an eyepatch: a world in which her personal injury is massive.

My vision is not excellent. And you detached my retina.

DANCER: Yeah, you reach a point where nothing's excellent anymore.

COBBLER: (*her hand*) See this? Punched a hydro pole. (*the Lover*) She made me mad. Can't feel this whole palm. Slap it.

DOCTOR: No.

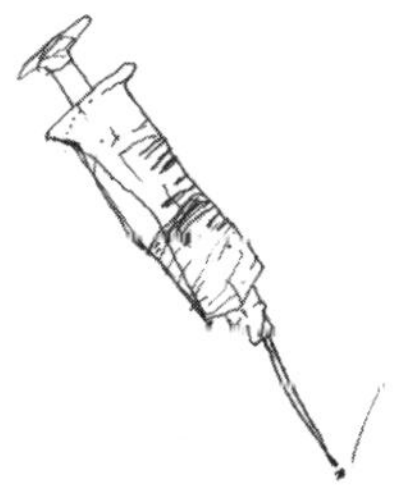

Seven: Pre-op Checks

DOCTOR: This is pre-op checks.

LOVER: What do you want from me?

DOCTOR: I'm checking your blood pressure.

LOVER: / This? What do you want?

COBBLER: / Nothing.

DANCER: She won't say what she wants.

LOVER: You want to see my shit? I'm going to put my shit on the table. All my shit. This is my journal. Here, read it. / This is small change. Twenty-five. Five, twenty-five, thirty-five.

COBBLER: / I don't want to see your shit.

DOCTOR: Your blood pressure is very good.

LOVER: This is a condom. Sensation. This? I don't know what that is, that's not even mine. This is my phone. You want this? Want to check my calls?

COBBLER: I thought you didn't pay your phone.

LOVER: I didn't. And then I did. I also broke it, then I fixed it. Then I lost it, then I found it. It's a phone.

DOCTOR: I'm checking your hemoglobin.

LOVER: Why are you mad at me? What the fuck's with sleeping with the fuck what the fuck it doesn't matter. You realize, it doesn't matter.

COBBLER: No, it matters.

LOVER: Then why would you do that?

DANCER: She's not going to answer for real.

COBBLER: I don't know.

DOCTOR: Your hemoglobin is good.

LOVER: There was nothing bigger than us. We were the most important thing.

DANCER: She's going to lose it.

The Cobbler has a tantrum. When she's finished:

COBBLER: Sonny.

KID: Yeah.

The Kid comes to the Cobbler's side. A pair in the aftermath of violence.

The Doctor checks the Cobbler's Rh factor in silence. Rh negative.

DOCTOR: You're going to need a RhoGAM injection.

We are all a bit worried.

It's fine. We do it in the OR.

Silence. The Cobbler takes off her eye patch.

COBBLER: You just left, no recourse to reason.

LOVER: What's no recourse to reason?

COBBLER: Like no course to get to the reason behind your madness. You are presumed dead. Does that not strike you as unusual?

LOVER: Listen. Are you listening?

A train goes by outside: a demonstration of how hard it is to listen in a distracting world.

COBBLER: Yes.

DOCTOR: I'm doing an ultrasound.

Lights dim.

Silence.

The Doctor ultrasounds.

LOVER: For some reason I had to go. Probably the reasons were many, I don't remember anymore, but I'm sure I left because I had to go. It is completely unclear if I survived even to this day. If you don't understand by now then there's no way I can explain it to you.

COBBLER: So I will never know.

LOVER: I guess not.

DANCER: We don't get to know a lot of things, ultimately.

Silence.

COBBLER: How's it look?

DOCTOR: Good.

COBBLER: I have this bad, crazy fear I won't qualify.

DOCTOR: No, you do.

COBBLER: Fear of impossible things. You know, you can't find it, you won't do it, I don't qualify.

DOCTOR: You qualify.

COBBLER: Great.

KID: What are we trying to find? Qualify for what?

The Cobbler's phone rings: distinctive.

It's the Kestrel's ringtone.

LOVER: (*taking the phone*) Lemme see. Nice photo. I'm just going to text.

COBBLER: I feel like I'm not qualified for anything. Like I'm disqualified for everything. I never know whether to keep talking. Like all the words I use are cancelled from language for being unpopular just because I used them.

Lights return to normal. Ultrasound is done.

DOCTOR: You're good to go.

COBBLER: Thanks.

DOCTOR: You can head back to the waiting room.

The Cobbler's phone is returned to the Kid.

LOVER: He says hi. General hello all round. Not enough time to talk.

COBBLER: Never is.

Eight: Anxiety About Water

The gang sits in the waiting room. Time passes. It's getting hot.

COBBLER: What time is it?

KID: Eleven.

LOVER: We need more water.

KID: The water's done.

DANCER: There's some in there.

KID: That's coffee.

LOVER: How can the water be done?

KID: That's all we brought.

DANCER: We're supposed to run out of water pretty soon.

KID: We have. In real life.

LOVER: How? There was so much water a second ago.

KID: Yeah and now it's done.

DANCER: That's how it's going to go. One minute you have all the water you want, the next minute –

KID: Sawdust horse.

DANCER: Sawdust horse.

LOVER: We've got nothing to drink?

KID: We've got coffee. And Coke.

LOVER: Now we can't use the pancake mix.

DANCER: Also we don't have toilet paper.

LOVER: Who packed for this trip? Who did this?

DANCER: Would have been easy to pack toilet paper. Just chuck it in.

LOVER: Who packed this shit?

KID: What? I do all the work around here. (*to Cobbler*) I do all the work around here and no one thinks I can do anything. And no one is paying me.

COBBLER: Yep. It's time to pull out all the stops.

KID: What are the stops?

COBBLER: Everything that's stopping us. Shit.

KID: What?

COBBLER: Fucking nothing. Nothing's stopping us, it's embarrassing. You need a job.

KID: I know.

COBBLER: You haven't even tried to get one.

KID: I learnt shoemaking. You said it's a career. I have a job, I just need to get paid.

COBBLER: Then you need to learn how to stand up for yourself. We need to go back to town with real skills, not just do our own weird thing in private.

KID: Fuck.

The Kid spits.

DANCER: How'd you learn to spit like that?

KID: My brother. He had a vasectomy. Not a vasectomy – well, he had a vasectomy but also a ... bowel resection surgery.

COBBLER: You need to learn how to talk.

The Kid draws on the Cobbler.

KID: I'm learning guns.

COBBLER: I can see that.

The Kid stands down. She drinks a two-litre bottle of Coke.

KID: Really elaborate leprosy. Rich face. Money face. Grey Cup Superbowl. I am the serial killer.

She pretends to make out with the Kestrel.

Every type of pussy – pussy pussy pussy.

COBBLER: She's in the shit right now.

Thunder. A fast-approaching storm.

Everyone in the tent.

LOVER: This is not a tent.

Rain beginning.

COBBLER: Everyone in the tent! It's my decision!

The Lover and Kid obey.

Gimme my hat, Sonny.

The Kid gets the Cobbler's hat.

DANCER: Kid, I'll be taking my hat.

COBBLER: Give me my hat.

DANCER: I will be taking my hat.

COBBLER: Give me my hat, Sonny.

The Kid gives the hat to the Dancer.

DANCER: Thank you.

KID: It's hers until she's done with it.

COBBLER: You can't change teams. Just so you know.

KID: Why's that?

COBBLER: There is no other team. Sorry to say.

KID: Yeah, well. I'm on my own team.

The Kid goes into the tent.

The sky opens up. Rain.

Nine: Suicide Letter

The Cordovan sisters side by side: the Dancer in her hat, the Cobbler in the rain.

DANCER: What do you think's the worst thing that ever happened to you?

COBBLER: Our parents died.

DANCER: No, it wasn't.

COBBLER: Yeah, it was.

DANCER: It was for me.

COBBLER: I was there too.

DANCER: No, I was there and you were a child. What's the worst thing that ever happened to you?

COBBLER: I don't know.

DANCER: Stop talking.

COBBLER: I was just about / to say something.

DANCER: / Start talking!

Silence.

Here's something about this. In the end, the good guy loses. He's misunderstood. End of story. No one understands him. They will not know you. They will not know you. Whatever you're doing right now, you're doing it all on your own. What is this, 'Where are we?' Wherever you are, you're there all by yourself. There's no we and it doesn't fucking matter where you are. That's all it's ever been. *Es lo que es.* Do you understand?

Silence.

Now, what's the worst thing that's ever happened to you?

COBBLER: Besides right now? Like besides today?

DANCER: Like ever.

COBBLER: You died.

DANCER: Read the letter.

The Cobbler reads the Dancer's letter.

COBBLER: Dear G. How are you? I'm doing good. I'm sorry I haven't written since I've been in Winnipeg. The ballet has taken a lot of focus. Do you ever feel like you inherited the family business and wasted your genius? I think it might be like if you chose a career in ballet and fucked your iliopsoas by the time you're thirty-one. I'd like to be able to say things didn't turn out the way I wanted. But I can't say that. I don't know if these things have been in me my whole life or if it's the things in my life that have made them in me. I'm writing you because some of the same things happened to both of us. And we are made of some of the same things. I do not wish to introduce a hanging into the narrative lightly. But I'm going to hang myself. I'm going to hang myself in this tree. This is your sister writing. Don't fuck this up for the family. Frankie.

The Dancer hangs herself.

The Cobbler picks up her sister's hat. Rain re-enters.

The Cobbler lies on the ground, the hat on her face.

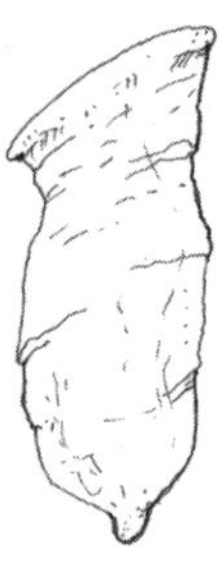

Ten: Q&A

DOCTOR: Okay. Let's take a little break.

DANCER: I died.

COBBLER: I know.

DOCTOR: Lights.

House lights on.

Let's go. Everybody. Have a seat.

The Doctor orders a whisky.

COBBLER: Can I get a drink?

DOCTOR: No.

COBBLER: It's not a real break.

They settle.

DOCTOR: How's it going?

They assess how it's going.

Who's got questions?

No one has questions, until:

KID: Who's Maxine?

LOVER: She's my dog.

COBBLER: She's part lab and part husky.

LOVER: And part terrier.

COBBLER: Really? (*It's true.*) Huh.

DOCTOR: Other questions.

KID: What's going on?

COBBLER: You're asking me?

KID: Yeah, what's going on? What's going on with you?

COBBLER: I'm having a life event.

KID: What is it?

COBBLER: Abortion.

The first time this word is used.

KID: What?

COBBLER: I'm having an abortion.

KID: You're pregnant?

COBBLER: Yes. I am currently pregnant.

LOVER: Yeah, I got a question.

DOCTOR: We'll take that in a minute.

KID: That's, like, such bullshit.

LOVER: I've got a question.

DOCTOR: We'll take that in a minute.

KID: That was my plan.

COBBLER: It's not as good as you think.

KID: This is bullshit. Why do you get to do everything and then you do it so shitty.

The Kid eyes the wolf pelt.

I've been wanting to put that on since the beginning.

DOCTOR: Go ahead.

The Kid puts on the wolf pelt. The Kid spits. Slow motion.

How'd you learn to spit like that?

KID: My brother. He had a vasectomy and also a bowel resection surgery.

The Kid is changed. It's the fucking Edward Snowden.

DOCTOR: What's your question?

LOVER: Who's the father?

COBBLER: There is no father.

KID: Obviously it's the Kestrel.

LOVER: Nothing's obvious.

DOCTOR: I thought that was obvious.

COBBLER: It's the Kestrel.

DANCER: It's just Kestrel.

LOVER: She knows.
What'd he say to you?

COBBLER: He said, 'Do what you want.'

LOVER: That's, wow. That's fair.

COBBLER: Very fair.

DANCER: Kind of all he can say, really.

COBBLER: Well, not really.

LOVER: No, not at all.

DANCER: Without being a dick.

LOVER: Yeah, but he's frequently a dick.

COBBLER: He's also allowed to have an opinion.

DANCER: Yeah. True.

COBBLER: I actually found it kind of offensive that he didn't have an opinion.

LOVER: A bit low on the commitment side.

COBBLER: Yep.

LOVER: But really. Do you want him –

COBBLER: No. Not really.

KID: I fucked the Kestrel.

LOVER: No, you didn't.

KID: I burnt down your house.

LOVER: Everett.

KID: I did.

COBBLER: Who are you, / ISIL?

KID: / I'm Everett.

COBBLER: You the fuckin' 9/11 Taliban?

The Kid riffs on current examples of global terror.

KID: Yeah I'm the fuckin' Boko Haram. I'm Anders Breivik, al Qaeda. I remember you before you left for the ballet.

DANCER: No, you don't.

KID: Yeah, I do. I was three but I remember you. You had a black leather jacket with a fur collar and you smoked cigarettes in a silver box. I saw you with that swimmer from Burlington. (*blow job*)

COBBLER: I've got a question.

DOCTOR: Yes.

COBBLER: Do you think it's okay to leave your best friend without saying anything – not a note, not footsteps in the snow – to never come back and be probably dead? Do you think it's okay to never speak to your sister for years after all the rest of your family is dead by horrifying accident and get her to posthumously approve your suicide? Do you think it's okay to put on a wolf pelt, whatever that means? Do you think it's okay to less and less understand what you're doing, to less and less see evidence in the world of even one small thing you believe in, so much unknown except that each day consistently brings some awesome new humiliation like getting pregnant by a notorious man with the name of a bird? Do you think that's normal or do you think that's just life, like, completely fucked up.

DANCER: Also, I have a question. Is it better for my sister's health to have a baby? I just heard that somewhere.

DOCTOR: That is impossible to say. But luckily we don't need to ask that question since an abortion is not a reverse pregnancy. She's not becoming a mother but she's also not becoming an astronaut. These things are both equal, in terms of health.

LOVER: She's not, like, done astronaut training, though.

DOCTOR: She's not, like, done mother training either.

LOVER: Yeah, but she's not sitting in a spaceship – that would be the equivalent. She's like a thousand steps away from being an astronaut, but like one step away from being a mother. One reverse step. She's not, like, not becoming a dinosaur.

DOCTOR: We're focusing on what she is.

LOVER: Right. What she's not is, like, vast and invented. I'm saying she's closer to becoming a mother than she is to becoming a moustache on a face.

DOCTOR: Right. Not becoming isn't a strong category. What we know is that she's a woman who's having an abortion. That's different from an inverse mother. Which is not a real thing. Whereas a person who's having an abortion is its own very real category.

We let this topic go.

Is anyone wondering why I'm not a man? Why the doctor is not a man? Or why your gang has no mens? Is anyone wondering if we've entered a world where there has been an apocalypse of men?

KID: (*man in the room*) He's a man.

LOVER: Those guys are all men.

COBBLER: Also, men don't have a lot of abortions.

LOVER: Well, they have abortions.

COBBLER: No, they don't.

DOCTOR: They don't that much. A Fistful of Abortions. For a Few Abortions More.

COBBLER: The Good, the Bad, and the Abortion.

LOVER: Brokeback Abortion.

DANCER: Dances with Abortions.

COBBLER: 3:10 to Abortion.

LOVER: The Last of the Abortions.

DANCER: Butch Cassidy and the Abortion Kid.

COBBLER: Dead Man.

KID: When were you going to tell me what I was helping with? Is this even legal?

DOCTOR: Of course it's legal.

COBBLER: It's covered by OHIP.

DOCTOR: It's just not very celebrated.

KID: This is so lame. Why don't you just be even lamer and have a baby?

COBBLER: You're going to get yourself killed in that wolf suit.

KID: I don't give a fuck. You can't even bear to hear your own name.

COBBLER: Like what? My name is Shia LaBeouf. My name is (*notorious man whose name is frequently spoken*). Why do we need to hear my name? Don't we all have sufficient concern for our own stardom?

KID: Well, I don't want to be here.

COBBLER: Yeah me neither. But at this point we can only go forward.

DOCTOR: Fifteen minutes.

Eleven: Feels Like Night

House lights out. The gang around the fire. 11:45 a.m. but feels like night. Thunderheads in the distance. The sound of a distant animal.

LOVER: What is that?

DANCER: I think that's a coyote.

KID: Yeah, or the fictional badger cat.

LOVER: What's that?

KID: Badger cat. He's not actually fictional, that's just his name.

COBBLER: We don't have that here.

KID: They think we do now. It's recent.

COBBLER: What time is it?

KID: 11:45.

COBBLER: Why's it feel like night?

LOVER: Daytime moon.

DANCER: That is the ugliest moon I've ever seen.

KID: Will you sing to me that song?

COBBLER: Yeah.

The Cobbler sings a corrido: *'The Legend of the Kid.' It is a made-up song about Everett's ways as a child, her promise as a young apprentice, and advice for her future glory.*

The Cobbler finishes. The Kid has fallen asleep. Quiet.

The Lover rises.

LOVER: I gotta go soon. Noon train.

The Cobbler nods.

COBBLER: Look –

LOVER: Only the germane.

COBBLER: He asked me if I wanted to come over for dinner.

LOVER: For sex.

COBBLER: He said dinner.

LOVER: What'd you say?

COBBLER: No. No way.

LOVER: Why? You don't eat dinner?

COBBLER: I often don't eat dinner. Also I had a lot of vegetables in the fridge that were about to go bad. Also I thought he meant sex.

LOVER: Right.

COBBLER: So then I didn't go. I mean, he ended up coming to my place.

LOVER: He went to your place?

COBBLER: Yeah. I had to use up those vegetables.

Silence.

LOVER: Did you kiss?

COBBLER: No. Not really. We didn't do anything non-essential. We basically didn't kiss.

LOVER: But you kissed.

The Cobbler nods.

Is that a yes?

COBBLER: Yes.

LOVER: Did you declare your love?

COBBLER: Like, 'I love you'?

LOVER: Yeah, 'I love you.'

COBBLER: No.

LOVER: And now?

COBBLER: Now?

LOVER: You still –

COBBLER: No. No no no.

LOVER: So what's your current romance?

COBBLER: Oh, nothin'. None. You?

LOVER: Lookin' at it. And my kid. Shit, she made you something.

The Cobbler is already wearing the necklace.

I don't know. She tried to explain it to me. It's a *milagro*. She's teaching herself Spanish. It's for protection.

COBBLER: She's heard of me?

LOVER: Sure. All the time. You've got the same fuckin' name.

The Lover looks at her.

You think we treated each other okay?

COBBLER: Yeah. You?

LOVER: Yeah. No one's going to get our story right.

COBBLER: Fuck, I hope not.

LOVER: Not you.

COBBLER: No. Probably not. Feels very unclear what's going to come true.

LOVER: Yeah. Unless it's painfully clear.

COBBLER: Yeah. One or the other.

Silence.

LOVER: Okay. I'm going to go.

COBBLER: Okay.

LOVER: Bye.

COBBLER: See ya.

The Lover hangs her boots. She begins changing into a nurse's uniform.

The Dancer rises.

DANCER: I gotta go too.

COBBLER: Yeah. Get out of here.

The Dancer removes her boots. She begins changing into a nurse's uniform.

You want to know something funny that maybe you don't know?

DANCER: Yeah.

COBBLER: After you died, they shipped your body back here.

DANCER: Oh yeah?

COBBLER: Train.

DANCER: Right.

COBBLER: Like, your sensei at the ballet. He sent you home. To me.

DANCER: Huh. I didn't know that.

COBBLER: I'm your only living family.

DANCER: Right.

COBBLER: I didn't bury you right away. I didn't have a lot of resources. Money or shovels.

DANCER: Yeah, that's okay.

COBBLER: Wherewithal.

DANCER: I know. What are you gonna do?

COBBLER: Yeah.

Well, I had you in the back, in the shed.

DANCER: The shed with the snow machine?

COBBLER: Yeah, snow-machine shed. And one morning I came out and it was like ...

DANCER: Breached.

COBBLER: Right. By like ...

DANCER: Animals.

COBBLER: Yes.

DANCER: Huh ... What kind of animals?

COBBLER: Nocturnal animals.

DANCER: Like owls.

COBBLER: Yeah.

DANCER: Cats.

COBBLER: Yeah, maybe.

DANCER: Fictional badger cat.

COBBLER: And mostly raccoons for sure.

DANCER: Did you –

COBBLER: I just let them have you.

DANCER: Huh.

Silence.

I think there's shovels in the shed.

COBBLER: I know. I'm sorry.

DANCER: That's okay.

COBBLER: I should have done better.

DANCER: That's okay.

COBBLER: I'm sorry I'm not doing better right now, for the family.

DANCER: You're doing good.

COBBLER: No. The Hashknives are doing better. The fucking Nacogdoches.

DANCER: Don't worry about them.

COBBLER: Lindsay Hashknife.

DANCER: Not of our concern.
I'm sorry about your eye.

COBBLER: You didn't do it on purpose.

DANCER: No, I did. I was repulsed by its weakness. But I'm sorry you still hold on to it.

Silence.

COBBLER: That ever scare you: what runs in our family?

DANCER: Yeah. Fear. Why, what do you think runs in our family?

COBBLER: I don't know. But it is fearsome.

Shift: night morphs into day.

It's like there are two seasons now. Normal and insane.
Where are we?

DANCER: I believe we are at an abortion clinic.

COBBLER: Thank you. That is actually so clarifying.

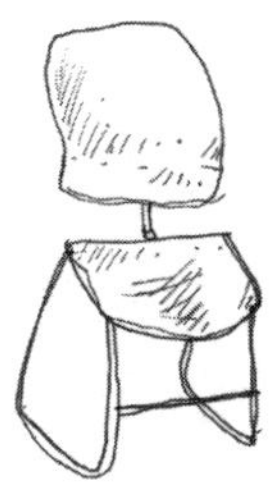

Twelve: High Noon

Sound of a train in the far distance. High noon approaches.

The Kid wakes. She rises and joins the Cobbler.

Train louder. The Kid checks the time.

KID: Yep. It's noon.

Sound of a train arriving into station, brakes, steam.

The Cobbler and the Kid look straight ahead.

Just the blood in our veins.

KID: Things seem so real here.

COBBLER: Yeah.

KID: Movies feel real but this is real in a different way.

COBBLER: 'Cause it's actually real.

KID: Yeah. I guess so.

COBBLER: You want to do what men do?

KID: Less talking?

COBBLER: No. Like, you know when you're a man?

KID: Yeah.

They nod, look off into the distance.

COBBLER: You've been a good friend.

The Kid knows.

KID: Things are going to be different from now on.

The Cobbler knows.

NURSE 1: ~~Grace Volonté Cordovan~~.

They say goodbye:

COBBLER: See you after.

KID: See you after.

NURSE 1: Follow me.

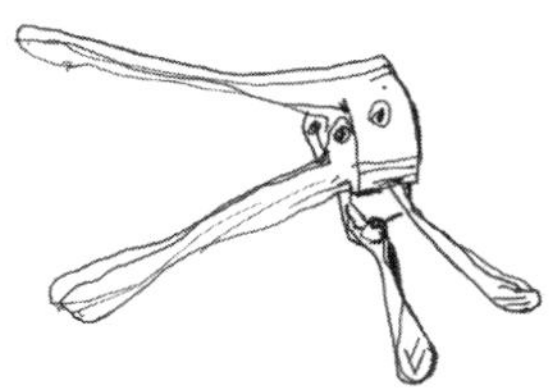

Thirteen: The Procedure

The space transforms for a clinical abortion procedure. The audience may need to move or stand.

Things begin going quickly. This procedure happens to the Cobbler. Her body is all-important and yet there is a sense of physical remove. Like any surgery, there is something between anxiety and abandon.

NURSE 1: Hello, I'm a nurse.

COBBLER: Hello.

NURSE 2: Hello, I'm a nurse.

NURSE 1: That's a pretty necklace.

COBBLER: Thank you. It's a *milagro*.

NURSE 2: RhoGAM injection.

NURSE 1: You have really nice hair.

COBBLER: Thank you.

NURSE 2: Tie her off at the wrist. Tap for a vein. Needle in the top of the hand.

NURSE 1: She's giving you intravenous pain medication.

COBBLER: Okay.

NURSE 2: Fentanyl: 50 micrograms.

NURSE 1: She looks so pretty in this part.

NURSE 2: Mix with Atropine: 0.3 milligrams.

NURSE 1: How are you feeling?

COBBLER: I feel dizzy. A bit nauseous.

NURSE 2: Feelings: normal.

NURSE 1: Hello, I'm a nurse.

COBBLER: Hello.

NURSE 1: I'm here to take care of the blood.

NURSE 2: Hello, I'm a nurse. I'm here to help with a bunch of other things that you won't be able to see from there.

Music: a Mexican boys' choir meets the howl of society. The Cobbler walks the length of the space toward her procedure, flanked by the nurses.

Stop time.

The Doctor is revealed in the operating theatre, in full dress and power, under magnificent surgical lights. She wears her bulletproof vest – rabbit and Kevlar.

DOCTOR: Hello, I'm the doctor.

COBBLER: How do you do.

DOCTOR: Hop up.

The Cobbler gets on the gurney and lies in supine.

NURSE 1: Calves in stirrups, legs high.

NURSE 2: Speculum. Steel pan.

NURSE 1: Tenaculum.

NURSE 2: Pull the cervix down and hold it.

NURSE 1: Antiseptic: Betadine.

NURSE 2: Apply to the cervix.

NURSE 1: Xylocaine. Ten CCs.

DOCTOR: Little pinch.

NURSE 2: Local freezing in a needle.

DOCTOR: You're doing excellent.

COBBLER: Thank you.

NURSE 1: Pratt dilators.

NURSE 2: Silver graduated rods. Start with thirteen.

NURSE 1: Thirteen.

DOCTOR: Breathe in.
And out.

NURSE 1: Fifteen.

DOCTOR: Keep breathing.

NURSE 1: Seventeen.

DOCTOR: Any pain?

COBBLER: No.

NURSE 1: Nineteen.

COBBLER: No pain. Just feeling.

DOCTOR: Good.

NURSE 2: Twenty-one.
Twenty-three.
Twenty-five.
Twenty-seven.
Twenty-nine.

NURSE 1: Thirty-one.

DOCTOR: Good. Don't move.

A communal breath: in and out.

NURSE 2: Suction.

Breathing.

Curettage.

A high tone: outside of time.

DOCTOR: There might be this initial shock. This initial strange feeling. What's strange is you feel normal, just exactly normal, like you could be any place, any time, doing any thing. What's strange is everything is simpler than normal, no other place to be, no other thing to think, nothing else to do except / just be still.

NURSES: / Just be still.

COBBLER: / Just be still.

Cut sound. Lights return to normal.

DOCTOR: All done.

The Doctor: everything out, gloves off.

NURSE 1: What are you famous for?

NURSE 2: Three minutes or less.

The procedure is complete. Everyone leaves. The Cobbler is alone.

The world stripped bare. Silence. Stillness.

The Cobbler rises to sitting. She swings her legs over the edge of the gurney. She sits in profile.

The Doctor rolls on a trolley of supplies.

DOCTOR: Recover.

COBBLER: Yes.

The Doctor leaves.

Fourteen: Recovery Room

Recover: to get something back that used to be. To make up or make good. To regain strength, composure, balance, or the like, of oneself.

The Cobbler stands.

She walks downstage with the trolley. Where the procedure was distant, now we are close. Theatrical naturalism. The trolley has all the supplies the Cobbler requires.

The Cobbler performs these actions as simply as possible, making practical deals with the body.

She puts on a pair of disposable mesh underwear. She removes the backing off a huge pad; it comes up to her waist both front and back. She sticks the pad on the underwear. Pulls them up.

She feels nauseated. She sits. She opens a two-pack of Premium Plus crackers. She takes a small bite. She's unsure. She opens a can of Canada Dry ginger ale. She sips. She is thirsty. She drinks the whole thing. She processes this. She is unsure if she feels okay.

She looks at some coloured papers: instructions for recovery.

The Kid enters with the Cobbler's backpack and boots.

KID: That was fast.

COBBLER: Yeah.

KID: How'd it go?

COBBLER: Good.

KID: Did it work?

COBBLER: Yeah, I think so.

The Kid is wearing makeup. The Cobbler notices but decides not to mention it. A coloured paper:

What's this say?

KID: Instructions. We got says things about cramping, bleeding, excessive bleeding, no tampons, no sexual intercourse, no swimming, no tub baths, no douching, no hot tubs, no hot dogs, no hot tubs, sorry, hot dogs yes, hot tubs no, and no tub baths, I already said that. I can read, I just don't enjoy it.

COBBLER: I know. Help me up.

The Kid does.

KID: Are those new underwear?

COBBLER: Yeah.

KID: They're nice.

COBBLER: Thanks. I get to keep them.

The Cobbler puts on her shirt. She pauses. She puts on her pants, belt. She pauses. She kneels and vomits into a bucket. A fierce amount of liquid. The Kid holds her hair. The Cobbler lets her. She pauses. She vomits again. She pauses, awaiting further verdict. She wipes her mouth. We're good. The Cobbler rises.

Let's pull up camp.

KID: I'm going to go do my thing.

COBBLER: Go do your thing.

The Cobbler watches the Kid go.

End naturalism.

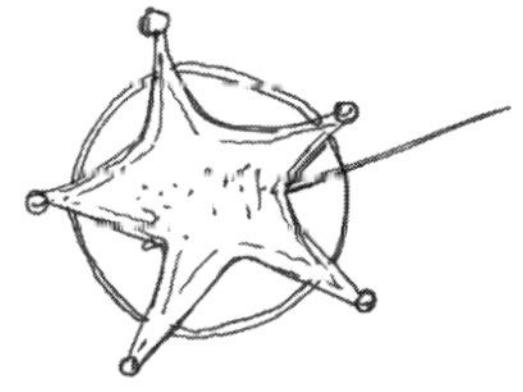

Fifteen: Fuck This Place

The Kid strikes the tent. She wields an axe and begins chopping the tree. Fuck this place.

The Doctor is there. The Cobbler is lacing her boots.

COBBLER: Just putting on my boots.

DOCTOR: Where are you headed?

COBBLER: I might head home for a bit.

The Doctor nods.

DOCTOR: This is Doxycycline, an antibiotic. Two pills. Take one in six hours and one in twelve, try not to barf it up. Don't soak through more than one pad an hour for more than three hours, you do that you call me. If there's a problem with you, you call me. If there's a problem with me, about you, I'll use the name Jane when I call.

COBBLER: What kind of problem?

DOCTOR: There won't be a problem. Also we did some STI checks.

COBBLER: You can just say it's you – I live alone. I mean it's a cellphone. It's a cellphone and I live alone. You can say anything.

DOCTOR: Okay. I'll probably say Jane.

COBBLER: Thanks. Thanks for your help.

DOCTOR: Yeah.

The Kid stares at the Wanted poster. She drops the axe, pockets the poster.

You should take my vest.

COBBLER: It's not my style.

DOCTOR: You should take it.

COBBLER: Okay.

DOCTOR: Put it on.

The Cobbler puts it on. The Doctor zips it all the way up.

Heroes can only look a certain way.

COBBLER: That's why I'm never going to be one.
Adiós.

DOCTOR: Adiós.

Sound of the tree falling, loud.

Sixteen: Showdown

The Cobbler and the Kid stand outside the clinic. We are in the city. Sound of a few passing cars.

COBBLER: Do we have change?

KID: Yeah.

The Kid texts the bus stop.

Three minutes.

Men heckle them sexually.

COBBLER: Can I have my phone?

KID: You'll break it.

COBBLER: It's okay.

The Kid gives the Cobbler her phone.

The Kid puts on leather gloves, produces the Wanted poster.

KID: I'm here to collect your life.

COBBLER: Come on.

KID: Five hundred dollars – it's a lot of money.

COBBLER: It's really not.

KID: Money or no money, your story's over.

Predictably, the world still astonishes.

COBBLER: You want to do this?

KID: Yeah, I want to do this.

Music. They ready for a showdown. A standoff. Cut music:

KID: I can't do this sober.

COBBLER: Since when?

KID: Don't you have some micrograms in your breast pocket?

COBBLER: They're antibiotics.

KID: That's fine.

The Cobbler gives the Kid her antibiotics.

Slow.

The Kid puts them in her mouth.

COBBLER: Gimme half.

The Kid returns half. They both take some antibiotics.

KID: This better not give me a yeast infection.

COBBLER: Naw.

Music re-enters.

COBBLER: There's something I should tell you.

KID: What's that?

COBBLER: I've got a bad temper.

KID: You've also got a bad eye, dry hands, and a good heart. You've just terminated a pregnancy under local anesthetic, and I aim to make five hundred bucks.

Music: a reckoning. A standoff.

Sooner than we think: the Cobbler's phone rings. It's the Kestrel's ring tone.

The Kid shoots the Cobbler in the chest. It's fucking loud.

The Cobbler still stands. The Kid still stands. They face each other, breathing.

The Cobbler falls.

The Kid stands.

The phone rings again. It's the Kestrel calling back.

The Kid goes to the Cobbler. She finds the phone. She answers it.

KID: Hello?
Hey. What?
Everett, yeah. What?
No, good, good.
Yeah yeah, nothing.
Oh. Yeah, it went good.
So what about you?
Oh, cool, cool, that's awesome.
Where are you? No, I mean what are you doing?
Cool. Can I come?
Hello?

The Kestrel has hung up. The Kid stands with the phone. She replaces the phone on the Cobbler. She removes her gloves and tosses them. The Kid stands. Imperceptibly distant: the sound of sirens or coyotes.

The Kid runs.

Stillness. Sound of the wind, blowing dust.

The Cobber's phone rings. No special ring, just an unknown caller.

With an intake of breath – full cast – the Cobbler's body animates. She sits up. She breathes. The phone still rings. Sirens are approaching. The Cobbler pats her chest. She finds her phone. She answers it.

COBBLER: Hello?
This is she.
Hi, Jane.
Mm-hm.
Mm-hm.
No, I'm still alive.
Thanks for the vest, by the way.
Okay then.
Mm-hmm.
Okay. (*STI tests negative*) Good news. I didn't really think I had those things. Right. Totally. Good to know. Thanks. No I'm going to walk. Not that far.

Sirens closer.

Yeah. No, it's fine.
I should go.
Okay, take care. Bye bye.

The Cobbler hangs up.

Police sirens upon us.

The Cobbler stands her ground.

The sirens pass. They are not for the Cobbler. Just another day in this world.

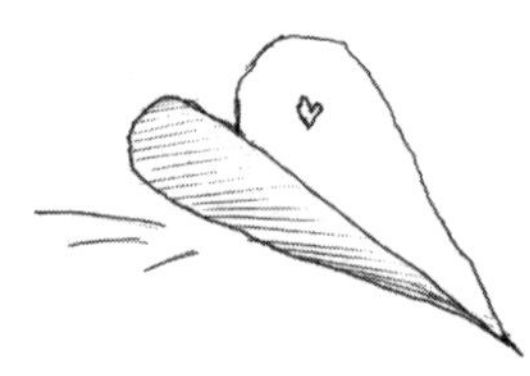

Epilogue: Movie Ending

Cut lights. A film is projected, light spilling over boundaries.

The Cobbler turns. She watches.

In the film the Cobbler walks home. She is unseen by the world. Just a regular woman who has had an abortion and now she's having the rest of her day. This is just our city, beautiful and normal as ever.

The Lover, Dancer, Doctor, and Kid are back in their dusters. We all watch.

The Doctor addresses the audience, over the film:

DOCTOR: That's it. That's the last I see of her. She never comes back. She does not return. Me standing before you: this is proof. This year the news ain't no different. Think, what's this bitch got to prove? Same thing anyone's got to prove. That this happened. That we were alive. That we tried to do good. Think, what happened in the end?

In the film, the Cobbler continues to walk until she becomes light. Stark white lumens. End of tape.

In the theatre, the Cobbler walks forward. Her gang all standing now.

The Cobbler puts on her coat and hat. She walks to the door. She stands at the threshold.

LOVER: What are you thinking about?

The Cobbler tips her hat. She exits the theatre.

The End.

Acknowledgments

The Supine Cobbler was made possible by the support of the Canada Council for the Arts, the Ontario Arts Council, the Toronto Arts Council, the National Theatre School of Canada's Theatre Engaging Communities Fund, and the Gallagher Foundation (in memory of Ellen Gallagher).

Thank you to Brian Drader for guiding this text with his special genius, and to Alana Wilcox for her invaluable input.

Thank you to Ker Wells, Anita Rochon, Claudia Dey, Karen Hines, and William Ellis, who believed, who wrote letters. To Rose Plotek and Amy Keating for their role in development. To Philip McKee, Mel Hague, Marina Mair-Sanchez, and Susanna Fournier for their insights. To Cecilia Conroy and Hamish Goodwin for their home.

To Len Falkenstein in Fredericton. To Arlene and Simone Leibovitch and the Morgentaler Clinics of Toronto, Ottawa, and Fredericton. In México, to Jesús Ramón Balderas Ramirez, Alfredo Pérez Cabrera, María C. Wayas, and Daniel Ellsworth. In Edmonton, to Kristi Hansen and Vanessa Sabourin.

Thank you to Bernadette Matos, Claudia Dey, and Heidi Sopinka for a magical livelihood. To David Anderson and the staff of Clay and Paper Theatre for their space. To Norman Nehmetallah, Jason Logan, and Lena Suksi for their hand in creating this beautiful book object.

To Austin, Dove, Kes, Soren, and Winter.

Thank you to Ishan Davé, and to my family, for love and unflinching belief. Thank you to the team of artists who created this piece alongside me – the most fearsome gang there was.

Jill Connell is a playwright, director, and producer. Her plays have been produced in Toronto, Calgary, Edmonton, Ottawa, Montréal, and Fredericton. She lives in Toronto.

Typeset in Albertan.

Albertan was designed by the late Jim Rimmer of New Westminster, B.C., in 1982. He drew and cut the type in metal at the 16pt size in roman only; it was intended for use only at his Pie Tree Press. He drew the italic in 1985, designing it with a narrow fit and very slight incline, and created a digital version. The family was completed in 2005 when Rimmer redrew the bold weight and called it Albertan Black. The letterforms of this type family have an old-style character, with Rimmer's own calligraphic hand in evidence, especially in the italic.

Printed at the Coach House on bpNichol Lane in Toronto, Ontario, on Zephyr Antique Laid paper, which was manufactured, acid-free, in Saint-Jérôme, Quebec, from second-growth forests. This book was printed with vegetable-based ink on a 1973 Heidelberg KORD offset litho press. Its pages were folded on a Baumfolder, gathered by hand, bound on a Sulby Auto-Minabinda and trimmed on a Polar single-knife cutter.

Edited by Alana Wilcox
Designed by Norman Nehmetallah
Cover design by Jason Logan
Cover inspired by an It Could Still Happen poster by Tala Kamea
Cover photographs of Katie Swift by Samantha Madely
Drawings by Lena Suksi
Author photo by Ishan Davé

Coach House Books
80 bpNichol Lane
Toronto ON M5S 3J4
Canada

416 979 2217
800 367 6360

mail@chbooks.com
www.chbooks.com